Signs

Signs

Poems by MARGARET GIBSON

Illustrations by Charles Chu

LOUISIANA STATE UNIVERSITY PRESS

BATON ROUGE AND LONDON

1979

Designer: Albert Crochet
Type face: VIP Trump Medieval
Typesetter: LSU Press
Printer and binder: Thomson-Shore, Inc.

Some of the poems herein have appeared previously in the
following periodicals, sometimes in slightly different forms:
*Back Door, Black Box, Feminist Studies, Hampden-Sydney
Poetry Review, Hollins Critic, Inlet, Lillabulero, Michigan
Quarterly, Minnesota Review, Nantucket Review, Painted
Bride Quarterly, Red Fox Review, Richmond Broom, Seneca
Review, Shenandoah, Southern Review.*

"Speaking Truth" is reprinted by permission of the *Hawaii
Review.*

LIBRARY OF CONGRESS CATALOGING IN PUBLICATION DATA

Gibson, Margaret.
  Signs : poems.

  I. Title.
PS3557.I1916S5   811'.5'4   78–11961
ISBN 0–8071–0493–0
ISBN 0–8071–0494–9 pbk.

Publication of this book has been supported by a grant from
the National Endowment for the Arts in Washington, D.C.,
a federal agency.

This book is for David.

And I want to thank, for their counsel and friendship, two who have always been generous and thoroughly indigenous—Louis D. Rubin and Dabney Stuart.

Contents

Signs: A Progress of the Soul

Spring Equinox

> In late March I wake
> fumbling for the quilt slipped to the floor.
> The limb of the redbud ticks on the house.
> A bird cries Cocoon!
>   Cocoon!
>
> Outdoors in my parka and boots
> I fetch wood for the stove.
> The sun thrusts its ram's horn
> up over the pines, butts against
> fencepost, pottingshed, pine.
>
> Sparks fly from redbud and walnut,
> the red clay harrowed for soybeans.
> I'm moved to stamp feet, shake
> horns, chant with my body, dance
>
> with the fire that streaks through
> these whips of raspberry, bloodroot,
> trillium, maple. Hallelujah!
> I cry,
>   I am here.

All morning I've been in the garden,
April, loosening the soil, turning it
feeling it warm between my toes.
I feel a tickle of roots in my feet,
an impulse to be the reaching downward
tap of the seed, to send down fibrils,
tuck around loose kernels of earth
knotting in and in.

I take the handplow, lean it against
my shoulders, push my weight
to the ground, turning up stone,
earthworm, chips of shell, rows
for bean and lettuce, hummocks
for squash. My body and the earth
meet in the blade
leaning together.

I go up for a beer and drink it
in the soybean field.
I watch the pulse in my belly,
remember the orchard after rain,
apple and pear blooms gravely stooped.
The bull in the orchard shaking
lazily his pearlhandled horns
grazing, in love with the pull
of gravity.

White petals from the apple trees
have unhinged, blown
into my hair. A high wind
riffles the river, May,
and I write letters to everyone
fold messages in bottles
steal into marinas to scrawl
bold words on sails. Words
want to take wind.

I tell everyone, listen
the world is a mirror
in which I see myself
coming towards
myself, never quite
closing the distance.
The one coming
to meet me has skin
like a mirror.
Often I cannot look
as the sun peaks
towards solstice.

I am restless
moved to dance
the two of us
risen in wind
just above the level
green wheat. I turn
slowly in pavane
slowly in love
court this one
I'll never meet
except in dance
but have always
lived with
as breath.

Summer Solstice

For my solitude I have this round
gazebo on the river's steep bank.
I have it screened in for long
tides of light, salt wind.
A solstice place for sun
fixed at its zenith, broad leaves
splayed to their maximum margins.

I have no use for the partial, the moon
quartered, a groping pincer in the night.
I need a home for the man and woman
inside me making love. A watery foundation's
best for a spirit at anchor with itself.
I feel smug.

After hours of picking peaches—
sunstruck—
I lie down in the grass,
don't know where I am.
Asleep in the sun, I wake
as I have for years
to a sense of light
to light
to light in the leaves
of these peach trees.

A child, I waked
once to a firetree,
a flicker dreaming out.
I crawled into myself
to find it, vanished.
Older, I walked
on the sun, a darkskinned
visionary attended by lions.
I saw this earth, spinning
in outer black space, turned
into paradise thickly planted
with lilies. I wanted
to get back.

From sleeping in the sun, July,
I wake to an earth hearth-hot.
I drowse, believing
sun is inside the earth
its center, the fire
orchard roots reach down to,
light which attaches us
to the earth, to the peach
to the flame-shaped seed
inside the peach.

When friends come, we agree
to work hard, make these stories,
our lives, just as we live them.

I want everything cleaned
up, linear.
I empty my mind
to blank paper,
rule it
straight—so.
Eat nothing
for days
but brown rice,
water. Keep
body fasted
pulled in thin
as bone.
Wipe tables
floors,
stack papers
screw lids on tight
throw out worn clothes
harvest, rake
put up the tomatoes
send letters, ask
What can I do
how serve
make amends?
I line up sins
examine
their labels
give up my attachment
to pleasure, ambition.
I want to be used
be practical
as this button
essential as salt.
Whoever's coming
I can wait.
I know what it means
to wait, to cut
through these hot
thick days
as the mower out
in the field
cuts hay
in a slow
analytical
sweep.

Fall Equinox

The sycamore blows,
yellow wind.
Wind drops.
Six o'clock
hush fills the river.
Last light
fills the bowl
of gold apples
and pears
on the kitchen table.
We are dancing.
Sun is crossing
the celestial equator
north to south.
It is falling.
Birds gather south.

Southing, autumnal
I follow the sun's arc
fall in love with you
dancing. You fall.
A wildhoney moon is rising,
evening tipping with weight
like a scale. Dancing
you are King David
joyfully coming home
dizzy with rhythm, falling
and rising with this wind
that shakes us, shakes apples
down, seeds
to the earth.

Today we tracked
wild bees to their hive
in the hollowing
windyellow wood,
brought home honey,
fruit of the falling
sun, elixir of pollen
and dance.
It will warm us
warm this kitchen
our dancing
through winter.

Cold. An unreasonable mist.
After supper I drink on the sly,
bourbon on the porch. Nobody's
here. I can just make out
the osprey's nest on the piling.
I'm not afraid of the dark.
I want you. Why aren't
you here? The osprey, mist
in its eyes, dives into the river,
renews its vision. So legend
says. And the phoenix
spices its nest, burns, dies
returns as a slender worm,
grows wings again, rises
again into the oarage of wings.
I think I'm a witch.
I died today three times
quickly, bright explosions
like sex, came back wanting
you to touch me all over
at once, river of you around me.
Will we ever be raised
incorruptible? I want
to be able to see to wherever
you are, look into myself, know
all the arguments by heart.
What am I hiding? Where
did I put it, the seed
the word that will sting me
back?

Dark, dark, dark.
There's always that blind
spot in the eye, part of the field
I look at, examine, can't see.
We must therefore keep
moving. Orion's my mentor.
The old ones who wanted me
to stay put forgot
to teach me not to believe
in revelation.
I put on a belt of hot coals,
stride through the dark.

Actually, we are together
reading the same book
in front of the fire.
We look thoroughly domestic.
There's a frost outside.
I'm tired from carrying wood.
Your hand's on my breast. Anyone
looking in should remember
the blind spot:
we're explorers.

I feel like the traveler
in the medieval woodcut
down on his hands and knees
on the earth, head
and shoulders clear through
an open seam he's found
in the cosmos.
I feel clear,
remember the blind spot
keep moving.

Winter Solstice

    Under a crust of snow on the field,
below the frost line, I think seeds
radiate like fireflies in thick August.
We're making bread
for Christmas,

speak of marriage as bread, our tenderness
as the only bond between elements
worth having. Water yeast honey
flour salt—
we watch the sponge

then heavy dough rise. Punch down.
Light promises fullness.
In love with this process,
kneading I use my hands carefully.
We shape loaves, brush them with eggwash.

As they bake, we walk the field
to the river. It's glacial,
midnight. I'm barely breathing.
Who knows what will happen?
Dark presses over the field

until it's hard not to remember
fossils, the earth, this pause
between upheavals.
The river freezes white. We walk
back carefully, feeling the height

of mountains curve in the pulse . . .
in the field, hidden energies . . .

Unable to sleep, I wander
through the house. 3 o'clock.
Outside, wind speckles with snow,
each flake an original word,
a world. In this room
amid rare books, an old pottery bowl
holds white African violets.
I water asparagus fern, speckled
angel wing, ivy.
I don't know what country
I've grown from. I am wind.

Where do we go from here?
asks the voice of the prophet.
Continents drift.
Faces of the dead
and the yet unborn
drift in my head.
Love drifts into dream
too distant from touch.
Think of a world with
no prisons, no prisoners.
I remember one man
a maker of words
who said simply,
Start from where you are.
Spread out. Nourish.
Reach. Be wind.

In early March we lie close under the quilt,
under a downpour rain on the roof.
Water fills us. We float. We are both clear
water, the glass bowl water fills.

This season, rain smells of earth and ice.
Winter and spring resist
equilibrium. There's nothing in you
I want to resist.

The glass cracks, we spill to the earth again
dreaming how to nourish seed stem bloom,
suffer our losses, return
born older.

Awake, we look at each other
as we might for signs of warmth,
the sun just rising in the river.

Tealeaves

Sitting here in the rain and morning light,
hair in my face, a rumpled nightrobe
pulled about my breasts, before the
morning paper after a night
                   of rock

and roll stars in the womb,
          I calculate my chances.

Tealeaves
          constellate and weave in amber
like words of famous men. I drink.
I think of poets who cannot rhyme at all.
                   I think
true prophets make the simplest statements
risk their hands
            and guts
                and balls
         on the turn
and counterturn of love. I think the stars
that sang on Plato's page rattle like dice
in our empty cups.

Lunes

O melon-bellied (I talk
to my gut) sweet
hibernaculum: it is time
to come undone.
I want to be empty, I want
to be clean as an eye.
I want an immaculate
suicide.

Lunation is exact to day
and second. I never know mine
until it happens: the cells
ring like wound clocks.
Who put the hex on me,
vengeance in the backbone
the doom of shrink and surfeit.
Lupercalian fatness,
moon-fruit.

A friend remarks
the primal tides swing in us,
blossom and seed, migration
of wind, sensation
of the turning season
deeply imprinted.
Such harmony, he says,
is perfect.

Screw perfection.
I'm a slave.
I'd rather be lacuna,
the breaking point in chaos
the zero, primal whore who
all by herself conceived
(to begin with)
perfection
          then time
                then light
                      then word
                      then love
and murder, murder
                then man
                      then me.

Forgetting

When you plant the Adonis pots for solstice
you cannot remember the names the seeds
will grow into. This has nothing to do,
you protest, with age. You know
the petals are white, greenish white
and gather in multiples of three.

Your dream of perfection, once exact
as an Attic frieze, slips out of mind,
in and out. You blame it
on the invading moon.
Whole undersea ranges
of your life

shift. There's an undertow,
tenacious. Once more you know
you've grown past yourself.
To steady, you reread an old novel
whose image of a girl's calm face
brightens in seawrack,

her eyes closed beneath a greenish purple sky,
a gull's extended wing. You wonder
why you marked some passages, not others
which now carve more richly
their delicate emblems
on your eyelids.

From the notebooks you consult, lists of a day's
work years back slip free, untidy
choices, relics. You say them through
like mantras, relinquishing until
they are invisible in the lamplight
and you are only

the moment, a casual nimbus,
a clearing where light gathers
green . . . white . . .

Revisions of the Familiar Face

I am sketching lines
about my mouth and eyes—
There's one rule
in this process—
I cannot
erase

One slip and that crow's
foot is a crutch—
Touch charcoal
to blank cheek—
there's a blemish

And behind my skin
in the dark—
chalk and a ghost's
hand move on the black
board of dream—

I am made of edges
and outlines

I can fast
and bones will edge
to the skin—
body will render
its hidden lines—
In the scan
of X-ray I learn
how I have swallowed
darkness in order
to be visible—

The face is
the only mirror
which depends
on a mirror
to see how it lines
and lies all ways
at once and records

the arguments
unfurled
in the cells
where the mad
lie down
in a helix
of chains—

This face
is a reunion
of relatives—
I press my hands
to my face
to touch
a kingdom—

ghosts
whose art is
blind palmistry—
a trace
moving inland
in the dark—

A Simple Elegy

I sew an Egyptian button
to a braid of black felt,
cord it about my neck.

Now I can talk about death.

An eight petaled blossom
carved on bone
protects me.

If the flower
roots
let its speech

transplanted

be love.
For I must speak
of death in this house.

I like to think we grow
our own bodies
that we choose our parents
not always wisely
but according to need.
I needed pain
and silence
as much as love.
I was richly
rooted.

The deaths in this house
make me think of gifts:

how many hours, afternoons
how many closed doors
I was given
as the big people brooded
outloud or cursed silently—
I planted acorns
pinned a riverfall of red leaves
to the curtains, stared at the stars

pasted to the ceiling over my bed
giving them the names
I would call my children
touching my body
its small knobby fronds
with pleasure
and with sleep.

God was a terror
the Godfearing family
put in my closet
at night,
a wind that rasped
out of nowhere
rattling
the coathangers.

I suppose they confused
God with Death.

Deliberately
in the morning
I confused my father
reading prayers
over the scrambled eggs
and buttered toast
with God

and my mother with God
when she baked bread
and sang alto into the oven
to make the loaf
brown and rise.

In the bedroom closet
God shook his skin
and bones.

At Christmas dinner the family
joined hands around
the heavy table
blessing it and numbering
all who were not there,
Amma who loved mince pie
Dennis who would have wanted

the wing, grandfather
who spoke the loveliest
prayer on the violin.
The preacher said
they were with us
un spirit. All flesh
is grass, he said, and I heard
glass, seeing all of us
suddenly in the lamplight
transparent figures
who could never hide anything.
We were all crystal and shining
and as the rest sang a hymn
of union for the living and dead
I wet my finger and ran it
around my lips until they rang
as clean as the tone of crystal,
Amen.

Years passed, marriages
rivalries. Gradually
my mother turned
the cupboard into lists
for her will.
She packed up glass
to save it.

My father grayed,
his mouth thinned
and turned down
as his mother's had.
A mole appeared
on the same plane
of his face as hers
and darkened.

I saw that the living
and dead sang hymns
together
but none of us
living together
sang.

As if ivy had furled
up the walls and windows
of the house

and into our mouths
covering us.
We lived in a hill.

Back for visits
I sat in the kitchen
with my mother at breakfast.
We broke silence
broke words.
We couldn't look
at each other simply

and say, "What matters
is right now, this hot
coffee, the oranges,
the cat rubbing
the leg of the table.
Don't be afraid."

I learned the deaths
of three distant relatives
long-distance.

"Don't come home," my mother
said. "There is nothing
really to be done."

There is.

I work the garden
bake bread
to give to friends

tell the man I love
I want to have children
make words, close distances

be able to say
finally
"Undo this button."

Glass has been broken.
Floors must be swept clean,
flowers rooted

in jars of clear water
windows polished
opened out.

Definitions

In a society unequally rich, the true materialist

braids onion and garlic to dry in the window,
oils her skin for work in the morning garden,
accepts drought, the difficult vine . . .

gives more than one meaning for *bread* as she sits
quietly that years may accomplish
with clarity their simple yeast . . .

praises the curled moustache of her lover's
intimate hair, his soft cockskin,
her own silks . . .

scorns distance and time, holds each moment
gently, absorbed with its particular
loud or quiet cry, its torn hand . . .

breaks wild wheat and cosmos for the pewter vase
without haste or impatience . . .

allows the highway its direction, mountain
its unoccluded prominence. Ground mist
she watches equally . . .

bows to dreams of the stranger, trembling, but gives
what is sleeping in the clear glass of the window,
what is waking in her eye her love . . .

She cracks each morning the brown, redundant egg
into perfect hemispheres . . .

The Way

always there is the road
bending through the town—
white huts, white stone
a road of chipped
teeth—
in the center
fountains
rise—dried roots
swing from the window
sills—there is no one
in sight

I shift awake
uneasy with myself—
the bookcase is packed
with scales and quills
of ancient birds—
if I look in the glass
I expect to be
a peasant pushing
a wooden cart
piled high with
brilliant gourds

Woman Writing

The woman writing
is transparent,
a magnifying glass
trained on the image
which stirs beneath
her gaze, as a stone
momentarily seems
a rush beneath clear
moving water.
She is an attitude
which gathers cress,
moss, emerald
dragonflies.
It is her own face
she watches, although
the stone only
has her attention.
She knows momentarily
the stone unfolding
its cities and roots,
its sky flight of herons.
Trusts that elsewhere,
held by her effort,
the rubble of stone
pitched on the edge
of attention, trembling,
holds off.

For the Sea, at Preston

1.

Last summer
inland, on the deck at evening
you called the light wind in the oaks
a sea breeze. I thought you meant
light, the low green evening and leveling
light which is the medium of birds—
that light
was a sea, that you acknowledged
the tidal sweep birds made cleanly
above us, the invisible radiance
Blake called choir of angels, praising—
that light
descending, a sea.

Wind
you explained, sea wind from the Sound
on certain evenings travels
over Mystic and Old Mystic, over feed corn
and the dust of Ledyard, through two century
stands of hardwood;
passes invisibly
between us, through us—unchanged
in its salt and kelp,
neither coarse nor fine as wind or light,
the sea
beckoning.

2.

I empty my mind and listen for green
cadences, taste salt
wind on sunburned roads.
A peasant in an orchid shirt
fades like a mirage into shadows,
long cedars of Lebanon.

    I'm dreaming your walk to Ephesus,
    your surprise at the sea's vast
    migration, old men
    and market tents where once
    sea stunned the city
    kneeling before it.

    My hands swim into dry light
    awake, in search of your body
    its fountains, your hooded
    mediterranean blooms.
    Whole continents drift,
    the sea cannot be held

        in Ephesus or anywhere.
        It rises in polar inlets,
        and I half believe our bodies
        rise to their close fit, their fill,
        as a lowland Chinese lily
        shatters.

3.

Sleeping by fits and starts
I see water, white
and wild collecting in the pond
wind hollows out between trees.
The pond expands towards Mystic,
a sea anciently obscured
by sunlight, rising at night
as dark webs of cedar before my eyes
shake loose ice gray terns
polar inlets and clearly
the dead whose arrivals and departures
once bit this ground so sharply
wheel ruts appear each winter
like furrows.

In the morning
I forget the sea, dark birds,
grief hard in the eyes of the dead.
Shells the children brought as gifts
nest blankly in porcelain cups.
Only when you suggest
clearing this land for a pond
will I remember
how Roman farmers
prayed before they entered groves
dug wells, or broke a consecrated dark.
The dream rises in my throat.
Words I would say
sink, terror
passes in a gesture so slight
you may or may not notice.

Without knowing why it is daily
a labor, I bow
to the sea.

Old Chinese Remedy

An empty day on Lantern Hill, where I sit
until the sea quietly, and the seagull wings
over the cliff's edge, move me with passion

that is not self-serving. I bring back
peonies for our bed, and we do the hovering
butterfly, joyfully balanced.

Again it's summer. Fields smell invisibly of plums.
The long-tailed phoenix and the jade moon
flourish in the east.

The Garden

March–August, 1974

Planting the Garden

Snow seeds the air

Warm in my parka I break ground
Earth gives

Clouds muscle by
A woodpecker knocks in the pine

I walk off the rows

measuring with twine
planting outlines   stake and string

I remember a grandfather
lunatic and blind

Earth he called *dulcimer*
Music he called *seed*

Asleep
he heard the echoes of roots

To greet him I traced the line
of my name in his calloused hand

He called me gardener
a signature in soil

I stitch the seeds of lettuce radish chard
in their shallow lines

The moon is the owl's eye
as I finish by dark the planting of corn

I think that wings will lift from this clay

Already I see one of them risen
perfectly white

The green one will tassle and cob
But the white one

the indigenous angel

will ripen in wind no man has felt on his bones
will release from its husk a covey of birds

sunfeathered   loud
and they will sing

Supplications To Make During Planting

Spirit of the Garden
hear guesswork

or if questions are prayers
these prayers

What are the names of the resurrection

Whose eyes have I borrowed from darkness

Why is it easier to come
            in the gaze of a stranger

than to come in the fields of desire
            to lie down in the head-high grass

                  that bodies may be wells in the earth
                  that sun may draw us up

                  that we may be the rain which washes
                  us clean   the touch of our mouths

What are the names of the resurrection

How can the soul be separate

Why don't you touch me

Why don't you speak

Dreaming of the Garden

All day I've weeded   raked
mulched the tomatoes with straw

examined leaves for flea beetle   aphid
prayed for the mantis

watered   thinned lettuce
planted garlic and chives in the lettuce

radishes in the cucumber hills
marigolds among potatoes

studied all day the natural balance
of growth and injury

Now I cannot sleep

In the sky I watch
the procession
Each woman carries
a yellow bowl
Each walks in a line
on the sun's rim
The road is
black stone
their footprints
fossils
I hear sighs
in the bowls

The bowls are heads

I see myself
walk to the garden
black after rain
Vines run
in corridors
Cabbages are praying
their leaves
folding over
and over
Under a stone
I discover a fist
in the shape of a head
I plant it
It grows into a spire
a spire in the body
of a woman
her feet drawn
upward
her arms weighted
with fruit
the intimate
cracks of her body
flooded
with poppies

I cannot sleep

I let myself out
The garden is cold
I kneel

to the spire
risen out of the skull
Her throat moves
a river
in summer

"Tell me what you understand"
"I don't understand"

"Tell me why you did that"
"I don't know"

"Tell me what you were once"
"I am bleeding"

"Tell me what you are"
"I am blood"

The Sun in Love with Itself

Weeks without rain   weeks
in a dry hex

Only the moon thrives
The air tightens

Voices prophesy
danse macabre

Mirages tremble

What I take for water
is distance

the blue sun of sandstorms

The only water here is sweat
and a wonder in the eye

of the waterbearer who must
be believing in pools

on whose skim of light
long-legged

green-billed birds reflect
and drink

Waiting for rain
I make stories

I am an old Chaldean

dreaming from a ziggurat
seams between stars

blueprints of ourselves
receding into distance

My grandfather traces
broken charts

Galaxies spin outward
like a fling of seed

In the last story I am blind
unacquainted with distance

I make a garden and love

lying down in the rain
and clay

making shapes
to take   to eat

Feasting

In a large skillet heat oil
add onion garlic   green pepper
When the onion is transparent
remove to a bowl   reserve
Add zuccini eggplant
Mix gently   Add onion
tomatoes   Sprinkle
with parsley basil
Season   Uncover
and cook   Serve hot
or cold to friends
Tell stories

In the ancient story
the woman Lotah
buries her lover's
head in an earthen jug
After two hundred years
she unearths it
brews it with herbs
anoints her skin
and drinks

Thereafter
music falls in the rain

rain falls in her dreams
from which she rises
shaking out seeds
from her fingers
the smell of sperm
on her skin
She is granted
the power to die
over and over

Revising this plot
follow the lines
of my face
with your hands
When we touch
we honor the dead
who have raised us
When we harvest
and eat
we are whole

The garden grows into our bones

A Grammar of the Soul

*While we sleep here, we
are awake elsewhere.*
Jorge Luis Borges

While I am on the dark bus and the spin of the wheels
    carries me into the crowded tunnel

she is rigid   awake under the scream of mosquitoes
    and one lightbulb bare in its socket

While I am sleeping in a sling between two palm trees
    which rattle in the trade wind off Cayman

she is hosing the blood off the sidewalks in New York
    after the accident   dreaming it green

While I am sleeping in a field of grass making love
    with you so that she will love me

she is in the mirror where it is snowing
    she is freezing to death

When I am unbuttoned in the cold winds of the hailstorm
    or blacked out in the cone of the twister

she pours a glass of cold milk and leaves it
    for me on the kitchen table

When I am dreaming that my body is pacing in the rain alone
    and drifting in the cupboard of a strange city

she walks down the other side of the street wet and
    smiling   She does not see me when I wave

She does not hear me when I call out for her to stop
    to tell me the name of the city

She cuts through the alley and enters the keyholes
    for she is wiser than I with secrets

While I am sleeping hard with my back turned
    she is writing a poem in my voice

She is lying behind me tracing words on my skin   words
    I will not remember in the morning

When I am pretending to sleep   my breathing a snare
    she tacks off on a reach   the jib sheet in her teeth

and thinks of heading south to a country where red
    chickens strut in the villages

When she is in the marketplace where the rabbits hang
        by their ears among strings of red pepper and garlic

I whisper how I have always been the stranger here asleep
        in your arms   restless and content

When she is sleeping with her maps and charts and lakes
        smoothed over her for cover

I am walking into the room where you are
        drumming your fingers on the polished table

While she sleeps waiting for me to leave you
        I decide to stay

Countershading

Sometimes alone, as now, reading quietly
poems or the newspaper
I'll see the sycamore leaves spindle
in the wind, in the gently moving
dark cedars, and in the room
out of the corner of my eye
there's a flicker, something moving
behind me on the left.

I know that it's you again
death, in your natural camouflage.
I've grown so used to you, rarely
you wink. Yet it's for you
the marsh bittern freezes still,
for you some pupa resemble thorns
caterpillers become sticks
the underwing moth a pattern of bark.

It's for you I wear clothes.
The human body's made to be visible
even the mottled ones. At night
undressing for sleep or for love
is like molting, a crisis
for which the loon retires
says Thoreau, to solitary ponds.
I know you're looking,
marking time
until there is a sere whistling
of wings, a flight in the dark
you will mistake for wind,
and I settle gratefully
down.

Speaking Truth

If I speak of the poem as a voice, my mouth
is a hive of bees. A line of them trails off
swarms on the walnut branch. Gather me.

Sometimes I am a gardener. The poems are beds
their bulbs dug up, split off, scrubbed. Touch them.
They have a noise inside them.

Let the old lovers, the bearers of speech, approach.
The hives round in neat rows. The bees return.
I place the tulips. They are real.

No fable, the bear's eyes prowl.
The constellation bleeds.
Inside each yellow eye mouths sharpen.

Surely I lie in these poems. I can deceive abstraction.
Lovers, when the tulips dry in bowls by the windows
I can deceive myself. I can say words I cannot know.

When you approach, listen.
Wear eyes as amulets. Watch.
I summon a helmet of stings.

Apples

I am peeling the apples making a note to replenish
the cinnamon. The knife pares in circles. The smell
of the peeling teases the air. I like doing this.
I like doing this alone. When I look out the window
the road stretches back in the distance heavy with dust.
The concord grapes, their bitter skins are blue.
The smell of horses and stables rises in the air.
I am on a fence rail looking down the road of dust
waiting for what returns after long absences. A
soldier in brown, this man who has always been missing
in action.

I am peeling the apples making a note that absence
is militant. The peelings huddle red and white on the
table, little slave bracelets. The man comes down
the road, tracks dust on the carpet. The man is the
knife that whistles at the core. I am Durer carving
the horsemen, hunger history ceremony rape. I put
the bracelets on my arms. I whistle. White wedges
of apple bake in the oven. Death is the heat. I will
sugar them, glaze them, serve them and eat.

Mending

There was a time I was content with fact.
He would sit with his daughters
and eat green apples with salt.
He would have other women.
Then I had to reconstruct the past
like the woman whose children's
worn sleeves made a quilt.
They grew past her hands, yet
she had them when she lay down
at night, provident.

I stitched, I tried
to thread the needle, I quit.
I turned my black thumb over
to growing vines. I read the dirty
parts of books so that I might chant
O son of a whore.
But they were not my words.
The blooms in the kitchen
coiled. Between the table's legs
a tiger stalked. Sufficient just
to watch it.

Illness and Idleness

All those I love are far away.
Last night the moon was full,
tonight it brims. *Amado mio*,
I have no familiar voices here—
gentle Po Chu I, Colette—no
music of the Chilean Resistance.
It is not good to be alone at night
without these other voices, although
no voice equals or dims the even dark
unwritten thrum in my slowed blood.

Why have I turned from your arms,
from music of the revolution inward?
My sleep is dark, steep.
I'm obscure, a slender
thread gathering force,
a ginseng.

Embrace

I drift to sleep
holding you
wondering
if the gesture
resembles
reaching

and wake knowing
the same
gesture
alone on my axis
turning
is dance

Lives in Translation

At eighteen, in his intimate notebooks, Flaubert
enters days when he longs to be a woman.
His flesh yearns, ablaze.
Other days, his pleasure
is thought itself, and art—
its strange translations.
His torment, the reversed
images of ourselves in mirrors.

"I now have only one name, my own,"
writes Colette,
her gardener's hand in lamplight,
admitting she catches the green
meteor, the blue night, but not
without distortion a beloved face.
Admitting her most essential art—
the domestic art of knowing
how to wait, conceal, translate.

As I study the lines of my body, its deft
histories, its one name, I'm drawn
near other lives.
I touch my sex with respect.
Other nights, nameless
I come to terrible simplicities,
not knowing whose hand, whose physical
labor, translates my life—
this blazing in darkness,
those scattered, astonished
cries.

Marks

Paging through old herbalists,
their simples of star grass root, willow
heart's ease, I draw a woman in the margin,
hunt wood sorrel on the stumps of trees,
brew mullein leaf and marrows
to counterbalance wind.

I mark thistles
in the sallet of old words,
enclosing them in hedges,
leaves: marking through Evelyn's
calendar, chaunting as the moon waxes
above his January parterre.
I write *to sing*: breathe deep.

Strict as I underline poets
I become an engraver. I study
firm black lines, there
the heart knotted,
here concern for clarity,
imperishable quiet.
In a ramble gathering roots
I learn that quiet
and silence are not one.
Quiet has leaves, sometimes
a throat. It is about to become
a thrust of breath.

In an old anthology
I mark *soul*, "a region
without boundaries," and *soul*
"a well-kept garden."
Closing the book, I dream
of garden wilderness,
the fresh snap of a radish
eaten just from the earth,
the dangerous beauty
of animals, their markings,
cries.

Rereading history
I draw bright confusions of seed
remembering Sartre closed
man's life as a ledger
each mark, each act of attention
added, each breathing in.

As I read, the pencil moves
also reading how Pliny takes equal pleasure
in box hedge smartly trimmed
and in knots of the plane tree, wild.
Underlining in green, I mark rows
for seed. In the margin write
soul: to breathe.

Yes, exactly. *Soul*,
the thrust inside the seed.

Wild Geese

The cold sea wind swells in from the shoals.
Dull green like a bruise gone numb and washing
out, the sea myrtle and the short scrub yaupon
lean away from the sea. Even when
there is no wind they pose on a veer
like the sea continually coming in.

Overhead, the water of wings and long
necks divides into geometric V's.
Cleanly the lead goose cuts through the air
and the others follow that line of least
resistance, graceful beyond their forms.

Birds

Migrant as sperm

they plane and glide
suspend all about me

A crowd of them strips off
a field

A pitcher of wings
tips over

Birds pour into the pine groves

All night
they send messages

Finally, you sleep

I don't know what
to think about love

When you come, you are plural

When we breathe out, we leave
ourselves for others

Above our winter bedsheets
I see birds flying

In the dream of my father
five fly out of his mouth

In Hong Kong a man tattooes
his skin entirely with black birds

In Munich a streetwalker
makes a wig of wings

Beneath chill galaxies
I see them flying

I've heard spores breed
in their droppings

pollinate human lungs

Our breathing gives riot
its roost

Whenever I sleep, I hear
the tentative pock

pock

the dent of waste on snow

The Deadyard at Merrifield

The plots are a litter of fake
poinsettia. The stones
have eaten the names out.
They are fat. Apples on the ground
are brown wrinkled sacks.

This is a still life. I expect
a sudden turning in the boxbush
to reveal the table of rainbow
pheasants, peeled oranges, the grapes
clear as children's eyes and green.

Against the deadyard gate
the wind humps
leaves like blankets kicked
to the foot of the bed.
I remember that I find
my nakedness in his face
as his hands uncover me.

It is winter.
In the broom field the wind
in dry straws sounds like fat
in a pan. My face burns in the cold.
I will never have children.

I begin to run.
I tear through the reaches of thorns
and they pull at my blood
my shoes may brim up with it
and I love it
I rage through the milkvine
the pods break
air bursts with the seeds
and fur gathers itself
like a great bear
damning the cold
and its hunger.

Crèche

Unwrapping this is our ceremony
of flight and pursuit. Our rite.
Why am I thinking of blood?
I am putting down cotton snow
for the crèche. She dresses the tree
with glass fruit from the attic.

She watches the stable
and fragile figures go down
by my hand to their old
places in this parable.
She wants to undress me for bed.

Why are we thinking of blood
as we sit down, finished
with trimming? I finger
the face of my watch, this glass
bandage, this telescope
on my rifle, the lens I polish.

              In this galaxy
black horses course in a pack
across snow. There could be wolves.

On the Cutting Edge

I try to imagine your death
the room
            the position of your feet
other people dressed in white
or black
            the timbre of your breathing

I break off a line
from Yeats as if I were snapping a green
branch from a bush for luck on the journey

in their stiff painted clothes, the pale unsatisfied ones

These are his magi
For me they are you
with your unrouged cheeks
                            your thin
silver hair with its faint blue tint
that hungry look
                        to your hands
as you sliced onions
on the white kitchen table
"Look" you say
                    pale and unsatisfied
"I want you to know how
to do this when I'm gone"

Death   the distance between
a slip of the knife
                        and your contention
that no one cared
You should have worn
                        painted silk
a backbone of stiff brocade in your shawl
You should have been able
to ask this
            Ease my death

Should you look down
to the foot of the bed
in that last unimaginable
room
      I will be there
      standing still
with a paring knife
and a silver bowl

onions in their brown
papery skins
          I will be there

Canticle for the New Year

I praise the earth
        which is no man's land and no woman's
        whose field is mined with bulb and seed
        whose calendar is grass

I praise the thunder
        which shakes seed from its pod
        swift clouds, the galloping horse
        fierce love

And the ditch at midnight, blood of the thief
        toil of the wheel in deep ruts
        into which rain gathers
        a bent moon

And the mountains, and you the watcher at the gate
        We listened to the black-billed
        bird fade at dawn

And I praise the wind
        which works its path into hard oak
        and birch, which sings in the fire
        released, a wind I can weigh
        consider whole

And the lightning of summer, withered tree
        at the pond's edge, landscape
        of starlings, wheat, swift
        insight

And the lake deep as dream, its riot
        of water, revelry of water
        the youngest daughter reborn
        in me when I laugh

In January, One Morning

the change in light alerts you—you want
a simple belief.
Blowing long steady breaths for fire in the kindling
you follow the ricochet of light moving in winged
shadows, as over water, continually beyond itself—
you realize the shape of light is its own
radiance.

Walking out past winter sumac in quiet fields
you find wind spread wide
and light—
last evening only a seam you split into wood—
spills from hollow pods, from each crack
and rent of this credible world, so clean
it suffices.

String

for Joshua

Ordinarily
I don't like knots
square or double—
they're tied.
Why else is Houdini marvelous?
why else do I say
"no strings attached?"

So I'm grateful
to a rumpled boy
whose hands sculpted
air with a mobius
strip of string—
as simple and profound
an art of making

as the roper's in Rome
the potter's in Egypt
the poet's—whoever ties
knots in string
to make an alphabet
for the blind.

I have meditated on string
and found it good—
the bowstring of taut
release, the bowstring
of resounding harmony,
the humility of string
in a string of pearls.

There's this fable: once
the dome of night
shone with stars aligned
on cords of light,
a web like the spider's
symmetrical, tensile
vast.

Whose careless hand
swept through it

no one knows.
We're blind mariners
reaching. Overhead
constellations, bits
of string, loosely
flutter.

Stars

for Megan

The flower is in the almond, I read
at breakfast—breathe *yes*
and move into a day of edges, surfaces—
lines of a poem trimmed
a walnut table polished to warmth
elsewhere breathing side by side
with the known domestic world,
barely touching.

With a child's eye in mind
I think to give you
paper stars for your ceiling
a glass to magnify the whorl of a flower—
and remember how one Saturday
you cut an apple into cross sections
to show me the star inside.

Now apples glow in the kitchen,
seeds are stars burning to flower.
You have given me a galaxy
of apples, the world as a nest.
When you sleep, secrets
inside you take fire.
You grow warm. New lives
dreaming inside you, shine.

Waking

Here is something to fight.
Even after sleep I wake crowded, thick
muttering the world.
                          Overnight the knotholes
bloomed. Now they pull in.
I have a ceiling, a glass door
a few certainties.
                          Overnight dreams leave
their tracks. I go out to delicate leafspurs
of frost on the blade of the bowsaw,
a flush through the trees, bloom
of peony on snow . . . and wood
must be cut
                    my mind must be wood
the branch ride on balance
the sawhorse steady, the bow
saw evenly through frost
and peony, wood.
Evenly, breathing evenly.
And the final kick of the foot that splits it free.

Remembering What I Want

Sometimes the room will darken and I'll hear
cries I know aren't birds.
Perhaps I've just read
how sandstorms took an ancient city
into hunger so deep there were no mice
left, no crows.

Or I've remembered Tolstoy said God
was the name of his desire,
and other wise men and women strove
for the act that left no trace,
pure as the sign of geese
reflected in a still pond.

That's when I'll echo what I least expect,
much as the taste of ale or alum, walnut leaves
or sharp camphor grow
mysteriously distinct.
I'll turn to myself and say, as if I were
someone else—

How can we be content?

Sometimes the room will darken, and I'll know.
Moments like these, they resemble walking
into the kitchen to boil water for tea
and, forgetting why I'm there,
I'll watch as my hand
finds paper

and writes down what comes,
if only my name.